tommy *noun.*

MAURYA KERR

POETRY

C&R Press
Conscious & Responsible

Cover art by Alessandra Baragiotta
Author photograph courtesy of Kimara Alan Dixon

C&R Press
Conscious & Responsible
crpress.org

For special discounted bulk purchases, please contact:
C&R Press sales@crpress.org

tommy *noun.*

When I get to where I'm going
I want the death of my children explained to me.
— Lucille Clifton

For my uncle Tommy and grandma Shirley, who I never knew; for grandpa, and especially for my mom. And for all those who began dying the moment their beloved stopped living.

Table of contents

Glossary

blood *noun* **1** the red fluid that circulates in and rushes from the arteries and veins of humans and other vertebrate animals: *Blood* wept from the wound. **2** persons related through common descent: He was their flesh and *blood*.

born *verb* **1** **a** — to come into existence as a result of birth: He was *born* beloved on a sun-filled spring day. **1** **b** — (be born of) to exist as a result of a particular situation or feeling: Her days soon became *born* of forlornness.

bullet *noun* a small metal projectile expelled from a gun: The dull thud of a *bullet* cleaving flesh.

bury *verb* **1** to place a dead body in the earth or a tomb: He was *buried* at dawn. **2** **a** — to cover or as if by covering with earth: His dog loved to *bury* her bones in the woods. **b** — to conceal from view: His mother *buried* her face in her hands.

dear *adj* loved very much: The dog was *dear* to all. *noun* a beloved one: Goodnight sweet *dear*. homonym — **deer** a hoofed woodland creature (family Cervidae): The dear *deer* startled and shot off at the scorching crack of the bullet.

definition *noun* a setting of boundaries; the stating of the distinctive nature of something; an explanation: She struggled to attach a *definition* to the empty space.

dog *noun* a domesticated carnivorous mammal (family Canis): The *dog* loved her boy. *verb* [with object] to hunt, track, or follow like a hound: Sorrow *dogged* her tread at every turn.

future *noun* a period time that is to come: Children have such a bright *future* ahead of them. *(Grammar)* a tense of verbs expressing what will be.

family *noun* a group of people related to one another by blood or love, such as a mother, father, and their two children: They were a *family* of four.

heart *noun* **1** **a** — a hollow muscular organ of humans and other vertebrate animals that, unless interrupted, rhythmically pumps blood through the circulatory system: Gunshot victims shot directly through the *heart* rarely survive. **1** **b** — breast, bosom: She placed her hands over his *heart*. **2** courage or enthusiasm: She lost *heart* day by day by day until there was none left to lose. homonym — **hart** an adult male deer: The hearts of *harts* were considered a delicacy by hunters.

mourning *noun* the deeds of grief over the death of someone dear: She grew gaunt with *mourning* sickness. homonym — **morning** the time just before sunrise; dawn: The *morning* brought fresh mourning.

muzzle *noun* **1** the projecting part of the face of an animal such as a dog: He loved to stroke his dog's soft *muzzle*. **2** the open end of the barrel from which a bullet exits: Point the *muzzle* of your loaded gun at what you aim to kill.

passed *verb* **1** to move in a path so as to approach and continue beyond something: He *passed* his life. **2** to disappear, go away: The sorrowing never *passed*. **2** to die (euphemism): Her son *passed* in January. homonym — **past** *(Grammar)* a tense of verbs expressing what once was.

prey *noun* an animal that is caught and killed by another: Hunters stalk quietly in search of their *prey*. homonym — **pray** *verb* to address a god or God with adoration, confession, supplication, or thanksgiving: The deer, a prey species, would *pray* to outrun hound and hunter.

Sirius *(Astronomy)* a star of the constellation Canis Major; the *lucida,* brightest in the sky; signifies scorching. — called also: the Dog Star, following at the heels of the constellation Orion, the Hunter.

squirrel *noun* an agile tree-dwelling rodent (family Sciuridae): The *squirrels* watched from above, alert. *verb* to move in an inquisitive manner: Every afternoon after school, he, his dog, and his best friend Timmy would *squirrel* about in the woods, often looking up.

boy, *n.*

the aim and fire
of a .22 caliber gun
by one *boy*
towards another

will result in
loss of life of said *boy*
instant and utter

scattershot heart
throb of a heart-

broke mother.

tom(my)

and how he loved to tell stories to make his mom
laugh and how lovely she
laughed and
her
laugh would make him
laugh so that they'd
laugh and
laugh and
laugh until she'd gasp out between
their
laughs 'oh what *tom*foolery! what *tom*myrot!' which made them
laugh even more and then some more
her talking fancy like that
until they both
ended up with s*tom*achaches or
in tears
or both

and when
she
cried
he
cried too like that time
she was chopping up *tom*atoes for a dinner salad and
cut her thumb
crying more from the sight of
so much
blood draining from her than from her actual pain

or the times his dad drank
so much

and
his mom always
waited until at least three pm to ask him to fix her
her *Tom*-Collins
even though he was too young really
with just the perfect splash of lime juice which
she drank on the divan in the living
room with a cigarette
waiting to be lit

but
he rarely
cried for his own pain
like right after his tonsillec*tomy*
but just before
he got to eat ice cream in bed
and watch *Tom* and Jerry
which his mom insisted was too violent
'a cartoon cat with a semiauto*tom*atic!'
to which he'd s*tom*p his feet and reply
'but there's not even any blood!'

or play Cowboys and Indians in his room
with his best friend Timmy
who
he loved and
who
loved
and let him
be the Indian with the *tom*ahawk and *tom–tom*s
instead of the Cowboy with a pistol but no bullets
just because his throat
hurt
so much

for three whole days

or study the ana*tom*y of dinosaurs
or tell scary stories about phan*tom*s
or wonder about exploding stars versus a*tom*ic bombs
then say to each other 'see you *tom*orrow' sadly

and how he loved his dog
who loved all
and feared none
except the stray *tom*cat who waited
in the bushes
at the bot*tom*
of the driveway
meowing,
insistent.

whereas, *conj.*

A cardiac penetrating bullet bears an entrance wound but no
        exit—tarry, root, rest, remains,

    whereas

a cardiac perforating bullet bores both entry and exit,
        ingress and egress, arrive and depart, come
           to go,
   here and gone.

dog, *n.* a —
family Canis

In the last few months of his life,
Tommy will love his *dog*
even more dearly.

He will ask his Mom and Dad for another *dog*,
to keep his *dog*
company while he's away at school during the day,
but they will say NO, and his *dog*
will be dead
within four months, although for reasons no one
would ever imagine,
even if pressed.

His *dog*,
who has no difficulty expressing
I love you freely to all, will,
when pressed,
admit she loves Tommy the most, will,
when pressed,
tell you Tommy is her best friend.

So, in the last few months of his life,
Tommy, whom his *dog*
loves most, will continue to love, deeply—
as deeply as
he is dearly loved.

born, *v.*

Tommy was *born* on a Thursday, died a Saturday.
On the first Thursday of Tommy in the world, the sun
rose at 5:06am and set at 6:43pm.

Tommy, *born* spring of 1954, dead winter of
1968, lived 5,021 days. Boys *born* that year had a life
expectancy of 24,345.5 days.

On the last Saturday of Tommy in the world, the waxing
gibbous moon rose at 9:28pm and set at 10:33am the
following day, a Sunday.

Tommy's mother, *born* a Sunday in June, would die
a Monday in October, too few days after the last
few days of Tommy in the world.

deer, *n.*
family Cervidae

mossy hush underhoove
                                 we rove
    flank a fallow line

       look
  up
halt
   hind tawny pelt   ahead
      winter
                       bough

scathe of crack   sulfur sound
     smell of red comes fleet fore hard
        still
      boy
    not night no Orion nigh
         still
              hounds of men ring
             rings of men hound
               rend

sing song soft before scream

             oh hollow harrow hell
                oh   god

preying, *ger.*

The smell of blood
>like marrow like root like dark like dirt like
rust like clot like *preying*
like

die.

Orion

My boy came into the living room and said, *Mom, you
are the hound, Dad is the hunter, and I am the—*

but he couldn't remember, so stood there, silent.
I wanted to know, but forgot how to speak, form

my lips into language, started to say *dear* or *hart* or *mourn—*
even though I knew that was wrong, knew I was

messing up words, but nothing more came out. In
the second part of the dream he tried again: *Mom, you*

are the deer, Dad is the hounds, and I am the hunt—
but then stopped, shook his head, started over.

No, you are the hunter, Dad is the deer, and I am—
and stopped again. *No, you are the hounds and the hunter,*

I am the dear. Then he walked outside into the woods,
the world. In the third part of the dream he was

standing in the yard, his back to the house. It was dark.
Too cold to be naked in the night—*he needs a blanket.*

He was looking up, still. In the fourth part of the dream
he looked back as if I had called his name, but I couldn't

have—I had forgotten how to speak, form my lips into
language. He pointed up and I saw him say, *Mom, see it?*

Orion! How I wanted to know, see it all, but I couldn't
get past his body—when had he lost his baby fat? Where

was my little boy's body? In the last part of the dream
he flexed and cocked his muscles, agleam beneath

the stars and said, *Mom, look, the Hunter!* And he laughed
and laughed and cried and wept, falling to his knees

in the cold dirt of a dark night.

The Mortality of Bereavement

Broken heart syndrome affects women almost exclusively

        the fatal force of stress hormones on the
        muscularity
            of her heart

meaning

        the welling up
        the weakening
            of a hart

meaning

        what once was
        what has passed
        what is no more

        the death
            of a deer one
    swelling the threat
            of her own death
    within one year of the death
            of said dear.

revolver, *n.*

remembering her second-born inside her
the pregnancy truly a long shot
such morning sickness
recoil from food
choke of bile rifling through her body
but such a small sacrifice for her new baby boy
armed with dreams
her prayers laid in the sights of God—
        please let this baby be the magic silver bullet to all
        my sad, and silencer of every worry—
her four-chambered heart set to burst
the blasting bright of her sun
aiming for highest sky
sure to shoot the moon
and she the *revolver*

meaning the one who revolves
meaning the one who spins and encircles
meaning the one going round and round and round

orbiter of his wake.

squirrel, *n.*
family Sciuridae

     we live small lives
          barely more than peep
show of

    green blade past winter thaw
         barely   bird nest
    speck
      of

       bright
   but on we do—black brambles ripe drip
acorn
    tombed to
      ground for
  safekeep   brown dew root
  beneath feet
    scrummy mulch
  between fur toes as we glee stomp or

         sad four-step
   to and fro
  to and fro
tawny belly
  words are flesh
 and
   flesh is fleet barely time to   sing to
    soft necks that wait or

    listen wide or

scurry
    courage boy

           darling   dearest
    unsung throat

for, *prep.*

1 a — indicating purpose: His father and uncles taught him that hunting was *for* sport and *for* fun, but the first time he killed a squirrel, sorrow snuck up his pant leg, into his bones, and burrowed in his belly; at that moment he knew men misled and fur might be love. When he couldn't sleep he clambered to his sister's bed *for* comfort. Afterward and in the wake, his best friend Timmy would come over and just sit in his room, *for* lack of knowing what else. House *for* sale. **b — indicating the object of (a) desire:** His mother liked *for* him to stay close to home. **2 being or constituting:** Not wanting to be taken *for* a coward or *for* too young, he walked into the woods, a brave and big boy, small *for* his age. **3 indicating enumeration:** *for* one thing, he wrote in a school essay a few weeks earlier that he was no longer afraid of death. And *for* another, he so loved his mother. **4 a — representing (the thing mentioned):** tommy, tom, my sweet my dear my heart my love were short *for* Thomas—his father's name, too. **5 because of:** We can't sleep *for* the sorrow, *for* the want, *for* the fear, *for* remembering and *for* not, *for* the dearth of hope, *for* the whelm of ache, *for* the salt and snot dripping down our faces into our mouths when we sleep on our sides, *for* knowing he must have fallen forward as the shot hit his heart when we lie on our stomachs, *for* seeing him blown backwards by the bulleted blast when we lie on our backs. **6 with respect to : concerning:** *for* bodies meant-to-love but not meant-to-leave, meant-to-sing but unsung. And *for* bodies too young, *for* bodies too lone, *for* bodies too little too lost and too tombed. **7 b — indicating equality:** Caliber *for* caliber. Parting *for* such sweet sorrow. Goodnight sweet boy *for* no morrow. **8 duration of time:** The sorrow like a slain squirrel that snuck up his pant leg into his bones and burrowed in his belly stayed *for* too long—or perhaps not long enough. (Because how long should one pay penance *for* wrest of life?)

His mother cradled him in those woods *for* ever, clinging to the dream that he was still alive even if just *for* a few moments after she found him there, in the woods, near the house. We visited his grave every minute, every hour, every day, every month, every year *for* years after he was blown and buried, killed and laid, rotting and forgone into mulch and hush.   **9   indicating place:** He left his house *for* the woods. He left his life *for* his death. He left quiet *for* quieter. He left air *for* dirt. He left sky *for* root. He left bud *for* rot. He left boundlessness *for* a box. He left upright *for* prostrate, plumb *for* prone. He left us behind, to fend *for* ourselves.

—not to be confused *for* its most common homonym, **four**: they used to be a family of *four*.

dog, _n._ b —
family Canis

                                       running—
    fleet fury foot
and I ran and I ran and ran
                run hart run bright

I ask for
        the muzzled shirt   they don't give it
                  wont
  so
I sit   wait
    still
   my boy
               barked

      they wept _dead_   but meant _look at the sky_
                    your boy as star

I sang _lonely_—they heard _give the dog a bone_
   when I roared _despair_   meant   _it's time_

        starry heel

          bury two
             me

                     running—

Mother Dies Eight Months and Twenty-three Days After Her Only Son

I'm so
afraid

my dear
boy

won't
recognize
me in
heaven

if

I'm old
and
wrinkled

when

I go.

entry, _n._

Does point of _entry_ really matter,
      in the end?

The "C" of Tommy's Secret Abecedary, Had He Lived, Not Shot Dead at Fourteen

cusp *noun.* on the verge of, as when laying
agleam in off-white rumpled sheets / frayed
borders / in dawn light / no one word laying
claim to the world / acrest, ready to unfurl /
overflow like the rollercoaster / where time
stilled / at the top fell quiet / at the top /
the forever of seconds, two maybe three /
heart-stopped high / so hushed / how
are you so beautiful / before rush of blood
and noise / throb of heart / before tissue
plummeting back into the fullness of here /
I am / here is my body next to yours / you
sing / ashine and laughing / oh beautiful
femurs / all the goodness of this / dusk this
life / take it furl it in to / our lungs our
hearts our open mouths / the claret force
of your tongue insisting / me insisting life /
let it be long remember / us / as you straddle
the cusp / look down at me, watching / you
like the moon, lit / whisper in to me / *wait
tommy wait / I'm coming.*

Afterword: Inheritance

a woman will walk into the first light of her garden   sharp early
air   a small cup of black coffee   held in both her hands   her
first of the morning   the break into dawn from dark silence of
night   steaming her vision   warmth when held close to her face
to sit wrapped in a well worn   down blanket   given to her by
her mother   who was given it by her mother and so on   and
on   in her favorite chair   the one placed both amid and apart
near and afar   of and not   in the garden soon to be overcome
by wild morning glories   *family Convolvulaceae*   a flower that will
seem the perfect solution   a flower she will choose for its feral
laureled promise   even though purple isn't the color she loves
merely likes   hoping   as she will   to complement the tinge
of the tall purple leaf plum tree in the back   *family Rosaceae*   a
species fast to grow but short to live   *plum* from the old English
plume   meaning   the part of an animal that resembles a feather
and she will think about plumage   her own   the collective
feathers of others   hoping   as she will   to fill in the cedar
trellis at the back fence   left behind by the former owner   a
man whose name she will not remember   whose mail will not
stop coming   whose children will keep calling   knowing in a
way that she   too   contains vacancies as vast as she is slight
so beautiful   opening themselves up as they do at first light
soon to discover that   while beloved by deer and swift to bear
blossom   morning glories will   one day   kill all plants in their
path   roots buried up to twenty feet below   giving credence to
their common name   *man under ground*   a name to give pause
such sorrow   she will murmur under her slowly warming breath
but knowing   as she does   that the dead are entombed at six
feet below   not twenty   a truth known in her bones   blood
bowels   a crawling vine that when innocently ingested by her
dog   a sweet   stout mutt   *family Canidae*   she will find in an
alley and adopt   a sound   steady pup   the living definition of a

dear   who will adore shortbread biscuits with a dollop of blood
orange jam   will make them both cry   her tears for his distress
with no words   his because he will worry he has disappointed
her with his raucous plant eating romp   *but how loosed and loved he
felt!*   his burnished   brindle fur soon to grey at the muzzle   a
twining vicious vine with heart-shaped leaves that entrench more
deeply when pulled out at the root   both noun and verb   rooting
lateral shoots up to twenty feet away   oh   the breadth of it all
and she will remember   as she sips her morning coffee   black
slowly cooling   something she read an evening past   something
she will finish tomorrow   about mourning doves   *family Zenaida*
the most ubiquitous bird but also the most hunted in America
over two million shot every year   one year seventy million   for
food   for sport   for fun   the mourning of its common name
due to its sorrowing coo   but most beautiful of all she will think
is the sound of their wings upon landing and takeoff   upon
coming and going   between land held and air borne   root and
sky   shore and sea   a form of sonation   meaning the deliberate
production of sounds   not from the syrinx   exquisite throat
of a bird   harmonic   but from other structures such as bill
tail   feet   feathers   wingbeat against wingbeat   such flutter
utterances of a body born   a body died   singing   no more sung

ACKNOWLEDGEMENTS

Thank you to my mom, for remaining soft-hearted and open to the world amidst such loss, and for sharing tommy with me. I love you.

Thank you to all the poets who have moved, taught, and inspired me—I am indebted.

Thank you to The Writers Studio and my fellow students in Kathie Jacobson's Masters Workshop—everything I know about craft, poetic rigor, and writing into tenderness I learned from and with you. An additional thank you to Kathie for her early reading of my initial attempts to gather these poems into a collection.

Thank you to Philip Schultz and T. J. Anderson III for writing about this work with such generosity.

And thank you to the following publications in which these poems, or earlier versions of them, first appeared:

Inverted Syntax: "for"
Chestnut Review: "The "C" of Tommy's Abecedary, Had He Lived, Not Shot Dead at Fourteen"
Vallum Magazine: "Afterword: Inheritance" and "Orion"

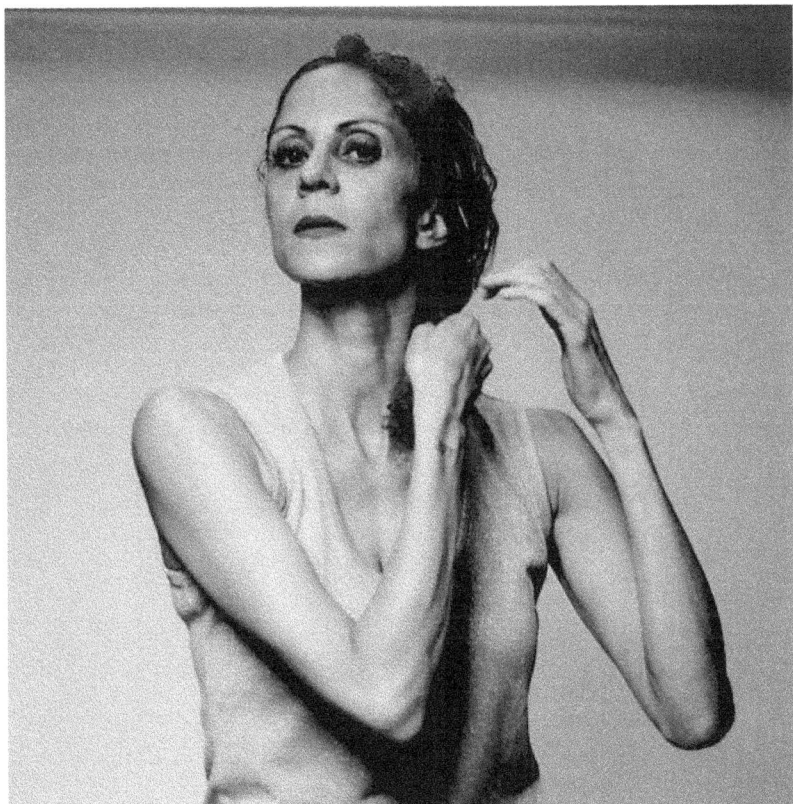

Photo by Kimara Alan Dixon

ABOUT MAURYA KERR

Maurya Kerr (she/her) is a bay area-based writer and artist. Her poetry has been nominated for a Pushcart and Best of the Net prizes, appears in multiple journals, including *Magma Poetry* and *Poet Lore*, and is anthologized in *The Future of Black: Afrofuturism, Black Comics, and Superhero Poetry*. She most recently won the 2022 Tom Howard/Margaret Reid Poetry Contest. Her first chapbook, *MUTTOLOGY* (Small Harbor Publishing), was published in 2023. Find out more about the author at tinypistol.com/poetry

C&R PRESS CHAPBOOKS

C&R Press hosts two chapbook selection periods from June to September and November to March each year. The Summer Tide Pool and Winter Soup Bowl Chapbook Series are open to new and established writers in poetry, fiction, essay and other creative writing genres.

2023 SUMMER TIDE POOL
The Consolation of Geometry by Alice Campbell Romano

2023 WINTER SOUP BOWL
Allison A. deFreese's translation from Spanish of Luciana Jazmín Coronado's *Dinner at Las Heras*

2022 SUMMER TIDE POOL
The Ice Beneath the Earth by Brian Ascalon Roley

2022 WINTER SOUP BOWL
tommy noun by Maurya Kerr

2021 SUMMER TIDE POOL
Rocketflower by Matthew Meade

2021 WINTER SOUP BOWL
We Face the Tremenedous Meat on the Teppan by Naoko Fujimoto

2020 WINTER SOUP BOWL
My Roberto Clemente by Rick Hilles

2019 SUMMER TIDE POOL
Inside the Orb of an Oracle by Dannie Ruth

2019 WINTER SOUP BOWL
The Magical Negro Reveals His Secret by Gabriel Green

2018 SUMMER TIDE POOL
Yell by Sarah Sousa

2018 WINTER SOUP BOWL
Paleotemptestology by Bertha Crombet

White Boys from Hell by Jeffrey Skinner

2017 SUMMER TIDE POOL
Atypical Cells of Undetermined Significance by Brenna Womer

2017 WINTER SOUP BOWL
Heredity and Other Inventions by Sharona Muir

On Inaccuracy by Joe Manning

2016 SUMMER TIDE POOL
Cuntstruck by Kate Northrop

Relief Map by Erin M. Bertram

Love Undefined by Jonathan Katz

2016 WINTER SOUP BOWL
Notes from the Negro Side of the Moon by Earl Braggs

A Hunger Called Music: A Verse History in Black Music
   by Meredith Nnoka

.

www.ingramcontent.com/pod-product-compliance
Lightning Source LLC
LaVergne TN
LVHW041205080426
835511LV00006B/744